COMPUTERS

What They Are and How to Use Them

Enslow Publishing
101 W. 23rd Street
Suite 240
New York, NY 10011
USA

enslow.com

Tricia Yearling

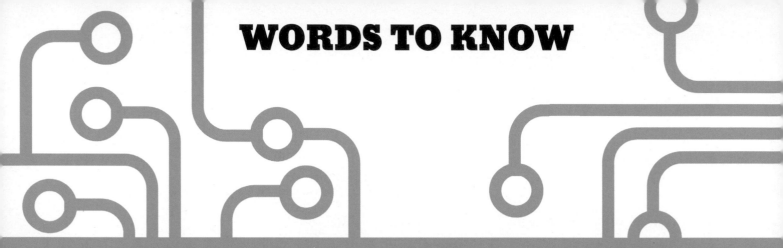

WORDS TO KNOW

abacus—An early computer made of string and pebbles or beads.

algorithm—Rules or steps that have to be followed to solve a problem.

application—A program that is designed for specific tasks.

browser—A program that lets a user navigate the World Wide Web.

commands—Codes or keywords a user inputs into a computer.

data—New facts given to a computer.

hard drive—Controls motion of hard disks, USB, and other storage devices.

input—Everything a user tells a computer.

operating system—Program that conducts communication between the various pieces of hardware, such as video, sound, and applications.

output—Data that has been processed into useful form.

program—A set of instructions given to a computer.

CONTENTS

What Is a Computer?

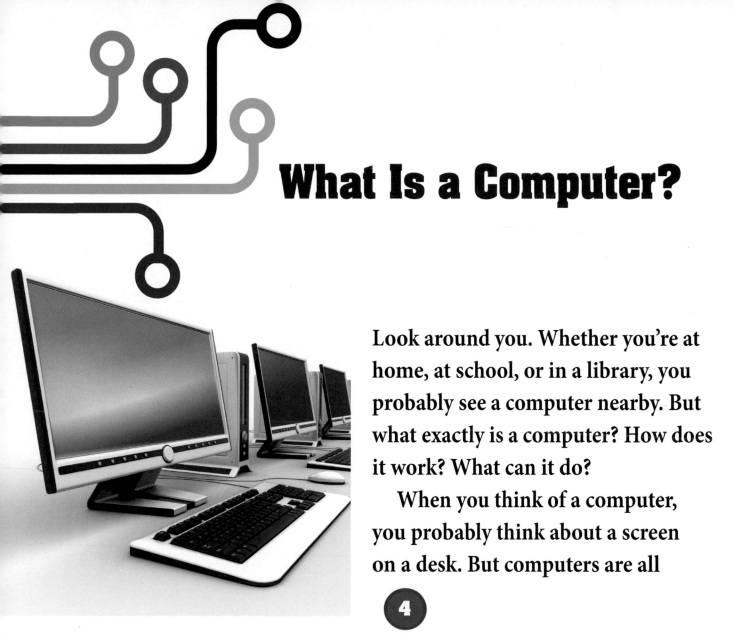

Look around you. Whether you're at home, at school, or in a library, you probably see a computer nearby. But what exactly is a computer? How does it work? What can it do?

When you think of a computer, you probably think about a screen on a desk. But computers are all

around us. We use them every day…
our phones, our tablets—even
microwaves, washing machines, and
TVs have tiny computers in them!

Long ago, before the days
of electricity or advanced
mathematics, computers were
simply people. Usually women,
these people computed, or
repeatedly made calculations,
and counted things like money,
distance, and tides.

This is a pair of ancient
computers.

All Shapes, All Sizes

Today, computers are everywhere and in everything.
PDAs, or personal digital assistants, are handheld

These days, most appliances have microcomputers, or very small computers, in them!

computers that can be used to create schedules, check email, and even take photos. All smartphones are PDAs, but not all PDAs are smartphones.

A PC, or personal computer, can either be a laptop, which is small and light, or a desktop, which is usually bigger and heavier. Supercomputers are big! They can take up a whole room. Supercomputers are the strongest, fastest, and most expensive computers on Earth. They're used for weather forecasting, engineering, and even NASA (National Aeronautics and Space Administration) has a few.

A computer can be used to do almost anything. On its most basic level, a computer is an electronic machine that performs the instructions in a program. It has four main functions: input, processing, output, and storage.

This woman is working on a supercomputer called the Cray-2.

A Brief History of Computers

Computers are older than you might think. The first computer was called an abacus. It was invented in Babylon around 500 BCE. It was made of beads and string. Unlike today's computers, an abacus served only one purpose: to help people count and keep track of things.

An abacus was used to count everything from crops to people.

In the 1600s, several inventors created early machines that would help develop computers. John Napier created a calculator that performed multiplication. German inventor Wilhelm Schickard created a calculating clock that ran on gears and wheels, while Wilhelm Leibniz created a calculator that could add, subtract, multiply, and divide.

In 1801, French inventor Joseph Marie Jacquard (pronounced JAK-ARD) created a loom. It was a

Jacquard's loom machine

machine used to weave cloth. It used mechanics to create the pattern in the fabric. The threads were woven through wooden plates with holes in them instead of by hand. This saved workers thousands of hours!

The Birth of the Computer

In the 1830s, English engineer Charles Babbage created all the parts that a modern computer uses. He made plans for many machines, but few were actually built while he was alive. It wasn't until 120 years later that his work would be used in mechanical computers.

In 1890, the US government needed help with the census, which helps count how many people are living in an area. By this time, there were so many people that they needed help.

Herman Hollerith created the Census Counting Machine. Punched cards, also modeled after Jacquard's looms, were fed into a sorting machine. Then they were read by the Census Counting Machine. This was the first time machines had been used in anything as official as a government census.

Charles Babbage created all the parts but never built his Analytical Machine. This model was built in 2014 at London's National Museum of Science and Industry.

Augusta Ada King, Countess of Lovelace, was considered the first computer programmer. She used her math skills to help Charles Babbage create blueprints for his inventions.

The Beginnings of Modern Computers

The computer as we know it wasn't developed until World War II (1939–1945). During this time, armies needed ways to communicate across long distances without their enemies learning their plans.

Many engineers, mathematicians, and

scientists worked on this. But it was cryptanalyst Alan Turing who helped the most. He created an algorithm and planned the Automatic Computing Engine (ACE) to break the Germans' codes.

Giant Computers, Big Results

In 1944, Harvard and IBM created the first programmable digital computer. It used vacuum tubes, which are made from glass and have circuits inside. It weighed 5 tons and used 500 miles of wire. The Mark I was 8 feet (2.4 meters) tall and 51 feet (15.5 meters) long. Its motor was turned by a 5-horsepower engine.

Arthur Scherbius invented the Enigma Machine at the end of WWI (1914–1918). It wasn't widely used until twenty years later.

Between 1943 and 1945, John Mauchly, J. Presper Eckert, and their team designed the first electric general-purpose computer. It was called the ENIAC (Electrical Numerical Integrator and Calculator).

In the 1970s the PC, or personal computer, was introduced. The first Intel computer hit the shelves in 1971. Macintosh followed with the Apple computer in 1977. Since then, computers have gotten smaller, lighter, and more powerful.

The ENIAC was the first computer that served a similar purpose to our computers today.

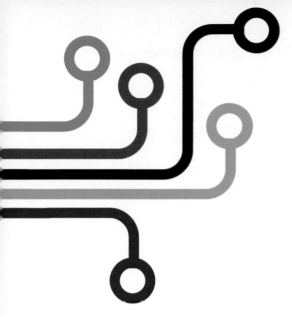

Parts of the Modern Computer

Today's computers help us communicate, research, create graphics, play games, and so much more!

Input and Output

Input is everything we tell a computer. This includes data, or the raw facts given to the computer. Programs are a set of instructions that direct the computer. Commands are codes or keywords a user inputs into a computer. These are directions,

such as update software. User response is any answer given to a computer, like Yes, No, Cancel, and Agree.

Input devices are important for using computers. Input devices include the computer's mouse and keyboard. These help us tell a computer what to do.

Output is the data that has been processed into useful form. Output includes hardcopy, which is a copy of something you can hold in your hand—usually printed paper—and softcopy, which means that it is displayed on a

Anything that gives your computer instructions, such as a keyboard or a mouse, is an input device.

screen. Output could be anything from text documents to graphics or even videos and music.

Storage

Storage is another important job of computers. Today's personal computers must hold hundreds of thousands of pieces of information: addresses, phone numbers, documents, photos, videos, and music. There are many ways to store this information. Main memory is the main storage on a computer. This keeps track of what is currently in use or whatever you are working on at that moment. For this, computers use RAM, or Random Access Memory. Remember to save your work when using this kind of memory or you will lose it when the computer is turned off!

17

Secondary or auxiliary storage is what happens after you save your work. This is used for anything that isn't immediately needed, such as addresses, data from the day before, or last year's bake sale records.

There are many ways to store electronically. Many people like to store their data in a way that they can carry with them. External hard drives or USB flash drives are common. They can be inserted into any computer so data can easily be transferred.

Internet storage is also common. These include the Cloud, Google Drive, and many others. The advantage of Internet storage is that not only do you have nearly unlimited space, but you can also connect it to almost any device. There are some debates as to how secure Internet storage might be.

What Can a Computer Do?

Every computer has an operating system. This is the program that communicates between the various pieces of hardware, such as video, sound, and applications. Windows 10 and Apple's OS X Yosemite are examples of operating systems.

Application programs (Apps) are designed for certain tasks. Tasks include word processing (Microsoft Word, Apple Pages, or TextEdit), spreadsheets (Excel), graphics (Adobe or Photoshop), or presentation (Power Point). Apps can also play

music, send messages, create video chats, and, of course, compute math problems.

The Internet

Of course, one of the most important things your computer can do use the Internet. Every computer has a browser, which is an application that allows it to browse, or look around, the World Wide Web. Examples of this type of app are Safari, Firefox, Internet Explorer, and Google Chrome.

Marvelous Machines

Computers are amazing. If you can imagine it, a computer can help you do it. They've come so far in just the past century. Imagine what will be accomplished in the next hundred years. Maybe you'll be the one who helps bring about the next computer innovation!

EXPLORING YOUR KEYBOARD

The keyboard is one of the most important input devices your computer uses. This is how you type in instructions for your computer to follow. To help you get the most out of your computer, knowing how to type is important.

1. *Look at your keyboard. You'll notice the first letters in the top alphabet line (going from left to right just like you read) are Q W E R T Y U I O P. The middle line reads A S D F G H J K L ; . The line below that reads Z X C V B N M , . / . The long key at the bottom of the board is the space bar. This is how you create spaces between letters and words when you're typing.*

2. *On your desktop, open your word processor, such as Microsoft Word, Pages, or TextEdit. You will see a blinking bar waiting for you to type something.*

3. *Place your fingers over the middle line of keys. This way your fingers will easily be able to reach all the keys. Place your left pinky finger over the A key. Your right pinky finger should be over the ; key.*

4. *Type the keys that your fingers are over. From left to right, the four fingers on your left hand should be hitting A S D F. The index finger on your right hand should be over the J key. The rest of your fingers will be over K L ; keys.*

5. Practice hitting these keys with all of your fingers. Your thumb will hit the space bar.

6. Of course, these are not the only keys your fingers will have to hit. Practice hitting the other keys on the keyboard while leaving your hand mostly in the same place.

7. When you type, the letters will automatically appear in lowercase on your word processor. To capitalize a letter, hit the **SHIFT** key at the same time. This allows you to make the punctuation marks on the top of keys. For instance, when you hit the **SHIFT** key and the ; key, : appears.

8. Now try some words. Perhaps type your name, school, or even your address.

9. Don't worry if you can't type everything perfectly. Typos, or typing errors, are common. And it takes a lot of practice to learn a new skill.

10. Now that you're familiar with the keyboard, it's time to use it! Maybe you should write a story. Perhaps it will be about your family, a friend, or an awesome day you had. Words are powerful and can help you create whatever you want. Knowing how to type them is an important skill when using a computer!

LEARN MORE

Books

Gifford, Clive. *The Science of Computers* (Get Connected to Digital Literacy). New York: Crabtree Publishing, 2015.

Owings, Lisa. *Stay Safe Online* (Library Smarts). New York: Lerner Publications, 2013.

Zuchora-Walske, Christine. *What's Inside My Computer?* (Lightning Bolt Books—Our Digital World). New York: Lerner Publications, 2015.

Websites

sciencekids.co.nz/sciencefacts/technology/computers.html
Fun facts about computers, RAM, ROM, and CPU.

sciencekids.co.nz/sciencefacts/technology/internet.html
Cool facts about the Internet.

bcls.lib.nj.us/Classes/Intforkids
Exercises to help master your computer skills!

INDEX

Published in 2016 by Enslow Publishing, LLC.
101 W. 23rd Street, Suite 240, New York, NY 10011

Copyright © 2016 by Enslow Publishing, LLC.
All rights reserved.

No part of this book may be reproduced by any means without the written permission of the publisher.

Library of Congress Cataloging-in-Publication Data
Yearling, Tricia, author.
Computers : what they are and how to use them / Tricia Yearling.
    pages cm — (Zoom in on technology)
Audience: Ages 5+
Includes bibliographical references and index.
ISBN 978-0-7660-7363-0 (library bound) —ISBN 978-0-7660-7361-6 (pbk) —
ISBN 978-0-7660-7362-3 (6-pack)
1. Computers—Juvenile literature. 2. Computers—History—Juvenile literature. I. Title.
QA76.52.Y43 2016
004—dc23
                    2015034035

Printed in the United States of America

To Our Readers: We have done our best to make sure all website addresses in this book were active and appropriate when we went to press. However, the author and the publisher have no control over and assume no liability for the material available on those websites or on any websites they may link to. Any comments or suggestions can be sent by e-mail to customerservice@enslow.com.

Photos Credits: Cover, p. 1 Denis Rozhnovsky/Shutterstock.com; Flat Design/Shutterstock.com (circuit board backgrounds and headers throughout book); p. 4 ©iStockphoto.com/arattansi; p. 5 Hulton Archive/Stringer/Getty Images; p. 6 ©iStockphoto.com/roey; p. 7 Per Breiehagen/The LIFE Images Collection/Getty Images; p. 8 Pavel Lysenko/Shutterstock.com; p. 9 Science Museum/SSPL/Getty Images; p. 11 De Agostini Picture Library/De Agostini/Getty Images; p. 12 Science & Society Picture Library/SSPL/Getty Images; p. 14 Time & Life Pictures/The LIFE Images Collection/Getty Images; p. 16 sergign/Shutterstock.com; p. 20 Blend Images/Shutterstock.com.